BUMBLEBEE BOOKS
EIGHTEENTH MONSOON

Ayaan Imran Shaikh is a young author and poet from Ahmedabad, Gujarat, India. He is the one among the natural authors who touch the soul with their decent efforts and elegant words directly from the books to the heart. Being a specialist in carving beautiful poems, he has launched his heartfelt poetries as the beginning of the journey to the novels. He is an expert in fiction long and short stories with good accomplishments in non-fiction areas too.

He is winning the hearts with his first-ever book 'Eighteenth Monsoon'. Ayaan is the one who doesn't only see the dreams but also works hard to make them true. His technique of selecting and settling the outstanding and elegant words makes him rare and unique from others. His other novels from the fiction and nonfiction areas are coming very soon.

Get in touch with him on Instagram - @ayaan_imran_shaikh

Eighteenth MONSOON

Words to your fragile soul

Ayaan Imran Shaikh

Published by Bumblebee Publishing
An imprint of Shree Balaji International
59, N S Road, 3rd Floor, Room No. 15B,
Kolkata, West Bengal – 700 001
Email: editorialbumblebee@gmail.com

Eighteenth Monsoon

ISBN Print Book - 978-81-949485-1-3

Illustrations sourced by the Author.

To your fragile soul.

CONTENTS

Part 1: Eighteenth Monsoon.

Poet in Hibernation

It's a time for me
To borrow a piece of sky
And fill my room with clouds-
The clouds of monsoon.
There are seedlings to sprout
Since when in my diary
Sown in late winters.

There are pages cramming
With pain-
With the pain of thirst
Craving for the shower-
The shower of poem rain.

The period has been halted
Since long away
The poet inside me
Is in hibernation
Skies are dripped heavily in droplets
Background is attaining
New colors of life
Earth is ready
for the downpour & fragrance.

Hey! The poet inside me
It's a time to open the eyes
To wet your words & body along
It's about to shower
The season's first rain.

~~~
~~~

Monsoon Curve

Breezes are the same
But there's something in it,
Making me love.
Everything is fascinating
my soul this monsoon
My feelings are reaching a peak
In this eighteenth monsoon curve

These wet evenings
looks so extraordinary
And humid day springs
Like it'll never come again.
Everything is incredible
In these mist forenoons
These eras look so rare
in the rhythm of the rain.

~~~
~~~

Drumming Droplets

The droplets were drumming
On my roof last night
Frigidity was bringing
My heart below zero
The midst of the rain
Delicately sensing the eyes
It's not easy for poets
To sleep in monsoon nights

"In the accent of rain
I've noticed a tone-
A tone of your smile."

~~~
~~~

A Proverb

"Icing on the cake"

Meaning;
You and monsoon.

~~~
~~~

Part 2: Romantic Melodies.

You me & tea...

My heart and the flame
Both were ready to be lit
One for the love
Another for the tea
A well romantic background
Two chairs & the Moon
Quiet night & dark hours

Prepared ingredients
-some tea leaves
& poems
Were ready to be cherish
One with the warmth
Another with affection
Two thirsty soul
And delicate lips
An evening in love
With wild countless kisses...

In these arrangements
You secretly arrive my mind
Take over the control
Of every beat of heart
You make me uneasy
Heat my body up
You kiss me so hard
Hug me so tight
When my cold soul meet
Your heated one
It drags my expectations
- a level up to the peak
Shift me to the poem land

And
Here the tea date begins…
Here the tea date begins…

~~~
~~~

Poet's Fuel

This accelerate the flow of words:

From poet's mind to the paper.

Menu

- Poems
- Love
- Hugs
- Kisses
- Care
- &
- Concern

Girlfriend of an evening

Once I was passing by,
A house enticed my mind of doubt.
It strained the vein of my imagination
The poem begins here it out.

There lived a brown eyed soul
Dawn of dark and delicate snaps
Of grey time in eternal spring
It was an ivory Tuesday
Of an immortal night.

All the fractured shadows
Were like blood in the fog
Completely incomplete
For the element of love
In these darling auras
Your breath was whispers in air
Settling my every corner of soul
Like the girlfriend of an evening.

~~~
~~~

Awaiting eternities

"My soul, city and monsoon
Even my poems are awaiting
Come soon come soon
My mornings, evenings & afternoon
Even my nights are awakened
Come soon come soon
Winters of January & summers of June
Even my spring seems faded
Come soon
Come soon... "

~~~
~~~

Isolated Emotions

I've jaded an age penning poem
It's a time to taste them
It's time to enjoy its flavor
Come someday leisurely
Out of my imagination
Will sit and spend a dusk
In each other
With sleepless eyes
With desperate heart
Coming up romantically
With our buried isolated feelings
Loving each other
Like we never loved before.

~~~
~~~

Musical Evenings

Theme of
Chirping little birds
Dulcet melody,
Soft sugary voice
And
Acoustic hymns.

These are the signature tune
Comes every evening
From that window
Fills the harmony in the air
Making everything,
Musical secretly."

~~~
~~~

Deadly Moves

My heart dipped in honey
Goes really mad,
over curves of your face.
My moon-loving eyes
Forget to blink lids
Around your silky curls.

Since you've said
That you love the moonlight,
I can't stop myself
To shine like the moon.

~~~
~~~

Part 3: Evenings in your Absence.

Wild Photographs

"You're quiet enough
To make hustle in silence
To enlighten my dark space
To enlighten the dark me.
It becomes heavy to handle
My obsession with moonlight
When you remain silent
And your eyes make me wild.
In the state of an evening
With your absence, my sweetheart
It's your silent photographs
Which creates a lot of noise."

~~~
~~~

Sleepless Nights

"Searching you somewhere in the sky
And settling you in my poems
Breaking the serenity of the dusk
I was making the noise
Through my up roared heartbeats.
This is how,
I spent my night
With the sleepless eyes
And desperate heart."

~~~
~~~

I was sitting in the garden; the cool breezes were singing lullaby in my ears. There were the droplets in the air. Everything seems to have changed. An evening was motionless. I went upwards toward my room, sat near the window with my diary. On every forethought, a new poetry was striking my mind with an image of your beauty. The clouds were gathered in the sky to shower on me and my pages.

Evening led to the night. No – actually the sleepless night…

~~~
~~~

"Not only your memories, dear
Your thoughts also keep me awake
Along with the stars
Along with the moon
Away from the people
Away from the world
Somewhere in my heart
Somewhere in you."

~~~
~~~

Canvas of Words

I sat to outline your portray
Neither with colors and nor brushes
I was filled with words
With an empty canvas
To sketch your smile
To catch your soul

There were some ballads and ode
Stained on it
Garnished with few verses and rhyme
Where, I coated your aroma
And sprinkled your essence
Which adorned the glamour
Which enriched the charm.

~~~
~~~

Letter to My Love

Your heart showers
An enormous love
Your eyes signify.
Your smile is the cup
Of a tea, my love
It gives me the wing
To fly high so high.

Hey spotless moon
You're only and only mine
My love is up to the infinity
And limitless to define.

You're my love and life
You are my shine
Your elegance is too
Delight my dear
Your lips are like wine.

~~~
~~~

Empty Ahmedabad

DAY 1

Since you've been gone
How empty is Ahmedabad

You took the colors with you
Also, you've taken the spring
You left a silence in my city
And disharmony in my strings.

How empty is Ahmedabad
How empty is Ahmedabad.

DAY 2

Since you've been gone
How empty is Ahmedabad

The winds are desolate
Streets are awaiting
My heart seems
To be scattered
Which made solemn everything.

How empty is Ahmedabad
How empty is Ahmedabad.

DAY 3

Since you've been gone
How empty is Ahmedabad

My city is ravaged by your absence
Creased by your memories
Alas! Alas!
What should I say?
You ruined its comfort
You ruined its peace

How empty is Ahmedabad
How empty is Ahmedabad.

DAY 4

Since you've been gone
How empty is Ahmedabad

The welkin does not
Drizzle anymore
You've taken the clouds,
You've taken the rain.
You left me alone
With an ocean of tears
Emptiness in my city
And an unbearable pain.
How empty is Ahmedabad...

~~~
~~~

Not A Poet by Mistake

Writing about you is not easy
It needs some extraordinary gorgeous words
With incredible gestures
And tremendous expressions
To pen down such immense beauty.

These poems then make me wild
Trouble me during every midnight
Every letter wreak havoc in the diary
Bringing the terrible flood of words
Its disastrous horrible noise
Exerts all the comfort from my body
This makes me restless
More than ever

Writing about you is not easy
Every time when I think
About your glamour and my poems,
I become uneasy.
Where there is your
Terrific stunning elegance
And my charming lovely words
These two beautiful things can make
Anyone fall in love

I am afraid all the time
That the reader might
Fall in love with you.

Writing about you is not easy
I had to bear the displeasure
Of words,
Whom I could not settle in paragraphs.

~~~
~~~

Flavor of Love

I tried writing odes
I tried free verses
Oh, what the flavor of love is tasted
I just can't stop writing about it and you
I tried ballads
I tried lyrics
Oh, what the flavor of love is tasted
That all of this cannot fulfill my desires too

You in the crimson
and blue shade
Arrives and receive
Me in nightshade
Oh what the flavor of love is tasted
I just can't handle myself, let me tell you
Chilled moon, you and me
Poem Land and hot tea
Close the door of the world
Come in silently
Oh what the flavor of love is tasted
Wishes for your silence to talk to.

~~~
~~~

Eternally Yours

There is still that beautiful chair
Breathing till now
Still cherishing memories
Still fragancing with our love

It was calling out our tale
Which the world can't hear
Except you and me
It was making me breathe
Oh! those moments
Once again glimpsing it thee.

But started complaining in between
Fighting for not bringing
You with me
It was calling out repeatedly
Where is she?
Where is she?

Garden has grown old
But it's intimacy with it does not
We are restful in their remembrance
Our tale & the moments didn't over yet
Somewhere somehow
New lovers are living them
Recalling the love stories.

Settling and breathing
Over the same chair of us
Where we used to spend
The moments of love.
-secrets we confessed
-sorrows we concealed

They are alive!
They are alive!

~~~
~~~

Minutes with you

I remember our last twinkling
Those five minutes with you yesterday
I lived wholeheartedly,
I was giggling from the soul
I was speaking the language of love
And listening to your murmuring hush

You're the rare view of the morning
When the dusk and dawn meet
When the sun and moon meet
For a hardly unique moment.

~~~
~~~

Part 4: Diary Room

Dear diary,
Don't ask how was the day
My extremely tired body
Is cramming with incredible pain
Sighing heavy breathes
Drenching in sweat rain.

Now
All I need is
A serene, soothing night
With cold moon and stars
Delicately beautiful,
lavishly elegant and refined.

~~~
~~~

Dear diary,
Today it feels like the soul in me
Went in an interval of nap
I am empty with words.

The night is going without stanzas
Stars are twinkling without shine
It feels an evening like a year
When you go off without a single para.

~~~
~~~

Dear diary,
I'm standing here
In the veranda
Hearing The birds
Talking to air...

Sensing this chaos climate
Once in a blue Moon
Where,
I am enjoying all four,
seasons in a day.

~~~
~~~

Part 5: Sonnet Corner.

01

You're my coffee cup
In the redolent winter morning
I don't know, when in your eyes –
All those watery monsoon went
And when I lost exquisite spring.
Your beauty wrapped in cashmere
In the dusk with chirping of birds
In such a serene beautiful silence
Your dulcet murmuring words.
I don't know, when my dusk became dawn
In your custody
And when my days went in your arms
You're my only comfort zone
Where my heart soothes and remains warm.

~~~
~~~

02

When I will meet you
The day would be rainy
In an era of monsoon
We'll walk hand in hand away from the world
When the time would be ceased,
In the night with pinkish moon.
I'll be there with my amorist heart
For the canorous chorus of your beauty
There will be fragrance of petrichor in the air
With the voice of rain narrating earthly poetry
A delicacy in shade and little touch of heaven
Hey beautiful beloved, all the stars by your side
Hidden in your eyes, completely arcane.

~~~
~~~

Part 6: Expensive Desires.

Exotic Winter Night

Imagine you and me
walking hand in hand
The season is winter
In absolute dark night
Chilled breezes blowing
with the only light
Filling our hearts with love
in moonlight.
Stars clearly observable.

The sky is quiet
I am loving the Moon.
In this exotic night,
We are looking into each other's eyes.
residing in arms relaxing
Getting rid of tiredness
and all the woes and scars
In such a cold background,
Your eyes are reciting tales making me enter your world.
Where I am speaking your favorite poems.
And
We are lost
We are lost.

~~~
~~~

Seized moments

Your hand in my hand
and head on the shoulder
Under the oak tree
after the first monsoon rain,
with fresh and new leaves.
Fragrance of earth
&
Showers of poem
Dribbling on our hearts
Isolating the time zone.

~~~
~~~

Romantic Evening

In the shady dusk
When the birds go return,
With the sundown.
When the sky turn dark
And the day ends up
Fleeing silence and stillness
In the bustling busy down.

You and me
Meet somewhere in the
Corner of earth,
Belonging to the different world.
Where the breeze
Holds the fragrance
With the flag of love unfurled

You and me
Wrapped in desires,
Meet at the peek
When the dusk is growing, yelling our name.
Where I am as cold as snow
And you are like the glorified summer.
Melting my existence,
You're pouring me in you
Where we are resting in arms
Fortified in each other.

There's nothing to hide
Where every blink
Is narrating a tale,
When we look in each other's eye.
You and I,
Become crazy and heated
Comes to be uncontrollable,
When our obsession
Attains so high.

You and me,
From the different world
Ends up our meeting
In poem with the final rhyme.
Let's go back now
With some drops of tears,
And keen hope for next time

See you soon...
See you soon...

~~~
~~~

"Meet me tonight
Draped in stars
Secretly in my heart
Wearing the one that
You never wore before

With all desires & love
Which are isolated in our heart
Unsaid, unheard
That we never felt before."

~~~
~~~

I've Never Told You

I've never told you,
But I was fallen in love
- With you at first sight.
I've never told you,
That you're the beautiful girl
I've ever seen.
I've never told you,
Even if you're not mine
I fear to lose you.
I've never told you
That your single smile
Is enough to pour my heart
– With happiness.

Can I hold your hand?
Can I take you for a walk?
Can I hug you tight in my arm?
Can I feel your concealed warmth?
Can I drench into your deep quiet ocean?
Can I read your feelings and emotion?
I've never told you,
I want to take all your woes
And fill your darkness with shine
I've never told you.
I've never told you.

~~~
~~~

Sometimes I wonder

Sometimes I wonder
You're made up of stardust,
princess of paradise
Born to rule the sky.

Sometimes I wonder
You're penned by a lyricist
With sweet and innocent words
With fine rhythmic tune.

Sometimes I wonder
You're the thought of a poet,
heart of his poems and
Soul of his fantasies.

You're beyond my understandings
Beyond my imaginations
Softening my hard corners
You crumble my heart in parts.

~~~
~~~

Part 7: Glorified Rahat

A Little Tribute to Late Sir Rahat Indori

Part 1

There is much pain
Hidden in the Rahat's Gazals
The words are silent
But the meanings are up roared
Can shroud the reader's soul
Can scribble his heart and mind

The pages don't speak them self
But they speak so loud if heard
They are in search of their lover,
To be read ambiguously
And peep into the story studded along with the letters.

Some situations gave pain to the Rahat
Some gave calmness, some provided the happiness
Some made him desperate
Some made him wild
But Rahat wasn't the one who sit
He didn't want to feel them alone
In a very proper manner
He proposed some improper tricks
Pen down those feelings
With all his heart
To be felt along with everyone,
Who loves him and loves to read…

Rahat was so intelligent
Knew the secrets of immortality
Still living in his words himself
And ruling over the hearts
Is there anyone who thinks he perished?
You're the haters,
Who think it so...

~~~
~~~

Shab-ba-KHair

शब-ब-ख़ैर / شب بخیر

Goodnight,
May the night pass well.

~~~
~~~

Part 2

After a long era,
You came to meet me Rahat
The poems are still on the table
Come let's pour some magic in them
But keep this thing arcane
The World wouldn't know
Come hide in my thoughts
It's too cold out, blanket my poems
and take warmth

I've spent an era in writing the odes
Now you've come,
So let's taste them along
I am heavy enough to handle myself
Delicate enough to be broken
There are pages awaiting to
be pampered with your touch
Come along
Come along

The night is too fragile today
Rahat do not begin your words
Just glance at my poems with a sight of grace
And make them alive to come out and shout
That can break my silence
Which is dwelled so long

It's almost a midnight
Now you may embrace my verses
And get back in the winds
To the way to your shrine
the shrine of words.
Come soon come soon
I'll be waiting for you

Shabbakhair...

~~~
~~~

Part 8: City of Souls.

Intimacy with your soul

The smile of your face
Blocks the poet's heart
Showers the happiness in the air
As an artist beautifying the art.

I keep myself in the moonlight
When the world becomes dark
Like a pleasant winter night
I come at your door to knock
To take your soul for a walk.

It's your soul, not you
Yes, it needs poetic eye to view
I hold your spirit tight in my arm
And makes your warm soul,
Cool and calm.

Neither my soul is thirsty
And nor yours
Both are pure and immortal forever
Can't die of course.
Can't die of course.

It's my intimacy with your soul
Where our body doesn't
Have any role
Yes! My love is real & true
Hidden from the world
Known by few.

~~~
~~~

"Your soul keeps me warm
In the cool chilled night
It's your smile which keeps me alive
In the world full of sorrows."

~~~
~~~

Last Breathe

Part 1

The day when
I'll write my last poem
My dairy may weep
My pen might bleed

With the news of my death
My poems will acquire
A melancholic silence

When with my last words,
I'll complete my verses
My sighing breathe will declare

'The poet is no more
'The poet is no more.'

~~~
~~~

Part 2

I might find difficulty,
In breathing
When my soul would be
Ready to flit.

The sky will turn crimson
In a moonless night
When
I'll finish my
Last pages of life.
With some incomplete
Mysterious stanzas.

I'll spend my last hours with you
Recalling those every moment
I'll stare,
I'll kiss
Your eyes and forehead
With lots of love

'One last time
One last time.'

~~~
~~~

The breezes whispered in my ears
Asked,

How deep is your intimacy?

The poet inside me,
Replied

My entire world resides, in her single pure soul.

~~~
~~~

Daughter of The Moon

Let me introduce
You to someone,

There is a girl breathing
In my imagination,
Bearing a killer smile.
With deep blue eyes,
She exerts my soul
With her marvelous unique style.

Her long black hair
Depicts the dark sky
Fluffy clouds to hide her
Shining stars to prettify.

There's something in her tone
That drives me crazy
Her murmuring delicate lips
Are like fresh petals of daisy
From ear to the heart
It turmoils my every part

She's like the
Daughter of the moon
Enfolded with snowy veil.
Poured with the light
Filled with love
Residing inside me
Like a Juliet of my tale
And,
She is you.
She is you.

~~~
~~~

Love Jazz

I was very happy loving soul
Your stunning face did all wrong
Made melody from the strings of my veins
And turned my feelings in the song.

The winds that have embraced you
Are dragging my heart along
Blowing me over miles and miles
Chasing your scent so long.

~~~
~~~

"You make my words fly
From the paper to the sky
Fleeing in the air
Pampering me with care
It is the state of your thoughts
And memories
What it would be,
In real you
Oh! Providing stillness to my
Hustling-bustling heart
Embellishing my leaf like heart
With delicate love like dew."

~~~
~~~

City of Soul

Love never dies
It will be remembered forever
In my poems written for you
In your letters addressed to me
It will eternally remain young
On the barks of those trees
Where we carved each others name
In the gardens & tree shade
It will go on with breathes
In your and my shrine.

When our souls will be tired
Of the body one day
It will fly away so far
It can leave the body
But can't rid of -
the feelings evermore.

Goodbye goodbye
We will surely meet in the
'City of souls'
After fleeing from body.

~~~
~~~

Part 9: Quote Spot

idea

"I am not so curious about having 90% or 98%
In my mark sheet
I am more interested
In having my name
On the Wikipedia."

~~~
~~~

~~“I quit~~
I can do it.”

~~~
~~~

"A beautiful life is better than the beautiful face
Remember,
No successful person is ugly
It's your success which defines your personality."

~~~
~~~

"Hard work is nothing without patience
I've always noticed that
The excellent destinations
Have the toughest road
But believe me, it gives intense joy
Reaching it with patience."

~~~
~~~

"My journey is pretty difficult
But I can feel the day
When I'll be on my destination
When there wouldn't be an inch gap
Between my success and hard works

The day I will smile
And shout loudly
Yes I did it.
Yes I did it."

~~~
~~~

"Number of attempts have a greater value than the number of victories."

~~~
~~~

"Patience is the only weapon in the battleground of life to gain victory over the difficulty."

~~~
~~~

"It's better to do something than doing anything."

~~~
~~~

"Never challenge silent talents with your initial attempts of few days, might their silence have spent 'years' unsaid. Remember, years are greater than days."

~~~
~~~

"I've seen people flying on the sky with half initial knowledge – challenging the eagles without estimating the potential.

Learn to be polite while learning, silent eagles have seen numerous amateur birds like you."

~~~
~~~

Part 10: Idioms Area.

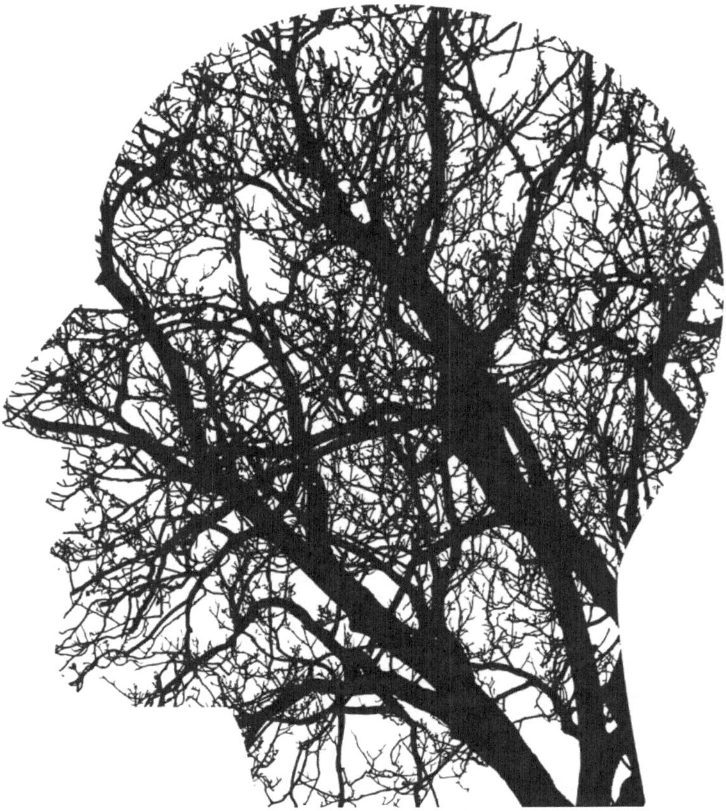

It's Just A Beginning

Night is young
Why breaking Out in A Cold Sweat
To catch out the breath
Have a sigh of relief

We've to go off
over a country mile
Fuel is full
Take ease on the driver's seat
Let's go over the moon
It's just the dawn of the life.
It's just the dawn of the life.

~~~
~~~

Tiffin

A significant dose of loaded happiness
And the pleasure in disguise
A box filled up with love & affection
Filling the soul's tummy

Oh, the unforgettable taste
-the taste of paradise.
All you can eat
Flavors as good as it smells
Worthy for the salt
Nourished with care.
Spiced up with the warmth
Finger-licking' good

It is Mouthwatering
Yes,
I know it well
which side of my bread is buttered?
My tiffin by my mom stands
Unrivaled & unconventional
Taste like you've never tasted
Unique as one and only one.

~~~
~~~

My Superhero

I've seen a superhero
Best of all possible worlds
Behind the closed doors
Do not bring the feelings out
To keep a low profile

Bestow everything under the sun
With no strings attached
He's light at the end of the tunnel
Who's never off duty
Around the clock

As nice as ninepence,
He's an unsung hero.
Of the movie of life

Let's make it simple
He's my dad.

~~~
~~~

Part 11: Free Verse Point.

"Your smile is too intoxicated
To forget
Too deep to come up
Hard enough to understand
Pretty easy to feel"

~~~
~~~

"Poetries can't be taught
What I do is
Putting all my efforts,
I inhale the words
Feel it inside
And exhale my sentiments
With pure and aesthetic feelings
Expressing you in letters
On the paper with some magic
And the handful of feelings
In the elegant moonlight
Assuming you as my moon."

~~~
~~~

Glorious situation:
"A poet in
gloaming twilight
With a cup of
A tea
&
A girl on the paper,
In the form
Of poetries,
loving each other
Secretly in the words."

~~~
~~~

"I won't love you
Till my last breathe
Because,
My body has not loved you
It's my soul,
And souls don't die."

~~~

"Your love is the wound
For which,
I don't need medicine

The more it pains
The more I get relief."

~~~

"Poetries are like heartbeats,
In the poet's heart."

~~~

"Only poets in the universe
Are blessed with an ability
To feel the soul
And I do of you
Along with mine

That has
Fallen in love,
Dissolved in affection,
Crumbled in fragments
Embedded in my void spaces."

~~~

"You made my soul love,
With your pretty cute smile."

~~~

"Do not keep your windows open
Because the wind that comes through it
Asks for a bribe to me
To go through my body
To illuminate my every part."

~~~

"These winds are addicted to my poems
Every time it deals with me
That if I shed the words in it
So, it will carry your fragrance to me
How impressive is the situation,
Both of us shine
After getting our special stuffs."

~~~

"If you allow me to hold your hand
I'll show you
How not to leave it
Till the end."

~~~

"I've poured my entire love
Into your heart
That the taste of my essence
Is well known by your soul."

~~~

"Love is something
Which turns the
Biological structure of the heart
Into poetic one."

~~~

"Real love was felt
After you went yesterday
With a delightful goodbye
Making my night moonless."

~~~

"You're like my
Beautiful Sunday
Of the bored ugly week."

~~~

Love doesn't need
Any specific language well known
Neither a certain body
Nor any color or charm
It just needs a soul
And pure loveliness.

That is able to polish
Your rough coarse heart
That can make you smile
Even in emptiness with no reason
Remembering your beloved
With no serious expectation
But some gentle outlook of
Each others well being
That's all.
That's all.

~~~
~~~

"From feelings to healing
Those emotions are poetry
When the head is filled with worries
And heart becomes heavy.
The light waves of sweet breezes
And that delicate touch is poetry

Neither a philosopher nor a poet itself
Is skilled to define it
That undefined flow of words
In the poet's stream
Is the poetry
Is the poetry."

~~~
~~~

Recipes will be the same
But you'll miss the taste of my hand
You'll miss
the aroma of love
While the dishes will be the same
In your kitchen without me.

~~~
~~~

"I can notice
the moon giggling
Are you
still awaken?"

~~~
~~~

"Now I
Don't wish
To explore
You more
Because
My love is
Stirred well
In your blood,
Dissolved completely
In your soul."

~~~
~~~

Acknowledgment.

Firstly, thanking my parents Mr. Imran Shaikh and Mrs. Chandni Shaikh. Next, I would like to thank my sir who taught me poetry - Sir Joseph Mathew – The one who held my finger and built confidence in me, introducing me to the poem land. Then to the one who inspired me on every step and made me write and write – Sir Mohammad Ali Saiyed. I would also like to thank my publisher Bumblebee Publishing, owned by Raunak Agarwal. Finally, I would like to thank Neha Joshi mam.

The End.